Animal

written by Ann Lee

Contents

◯Harcourt

Orlando Boston Dallas Chicago San Diego

www.harcourtschool.com

All animals have homes.

Where is this animal found?

This animal is in the forest.

Where is this animal found?

This animal is in the desert.

Where is this animal found?

This animal is in the rain forest.

Where is this animal found?

This animal is in the ocean.
Can you find it?

Glossary

desert

forest

ocean

rain forest

Index